Lerner Books • London • New York • Minneapolis

This book was first published in the United States of America in 2005.
First published in the United Kingdom in 2008 by
Lerner Books,
Dalton House,
60 Windsor Avenue,
London SW19 2RR

Website address: www.lernerbooks.co.uk

This edition was updated and edited for UK publication by Discovery Books Ltd.,
Unit 3, 37 Watling Street, Leintwardine, Shropshire SY7 0LW

Words in **bold type** are explained in a glossary on page 30.

British Library Congress Cataloguing in Publication Data

Donaldson, Madeline
Europe. - (Pull ahead)
1. Europe - Pictorial works - Juvenile literature
I. Title
940

ISBN-13: 978 1 58013 329 6

Photographs are used with the permission of: © John Elk III, p. 3; © Robert Fried/ robertfriedphotography.com, pp. 6,15, 22; © Betty Crowell, pp. 7, 8, 9, 11; © Dan Buettner, p. 12; © Erin Liddell/Independent Picture Service, pp. 13, 26–27; © W.Jacobs/Art Directors p. 14; © Jacob Jasiniski/Visuals Unlimited, pp. 16–17; © A. A. M Van der Heyden/Independent Picture Service, pp. 18–19, 24; © S. Carmona/CORBIS, pp. 20–21; © Prisma/SuperStock p. 23; © John Kreul/Independent Picture Service, p. 25.Maps on pp. 4–5, 10, 29 by Laura Westlund.

Printed in China

Zoom! Where could you travel on one of the world's fastest trains?

The **continent** of Europe!
A continent is a big piece of land.

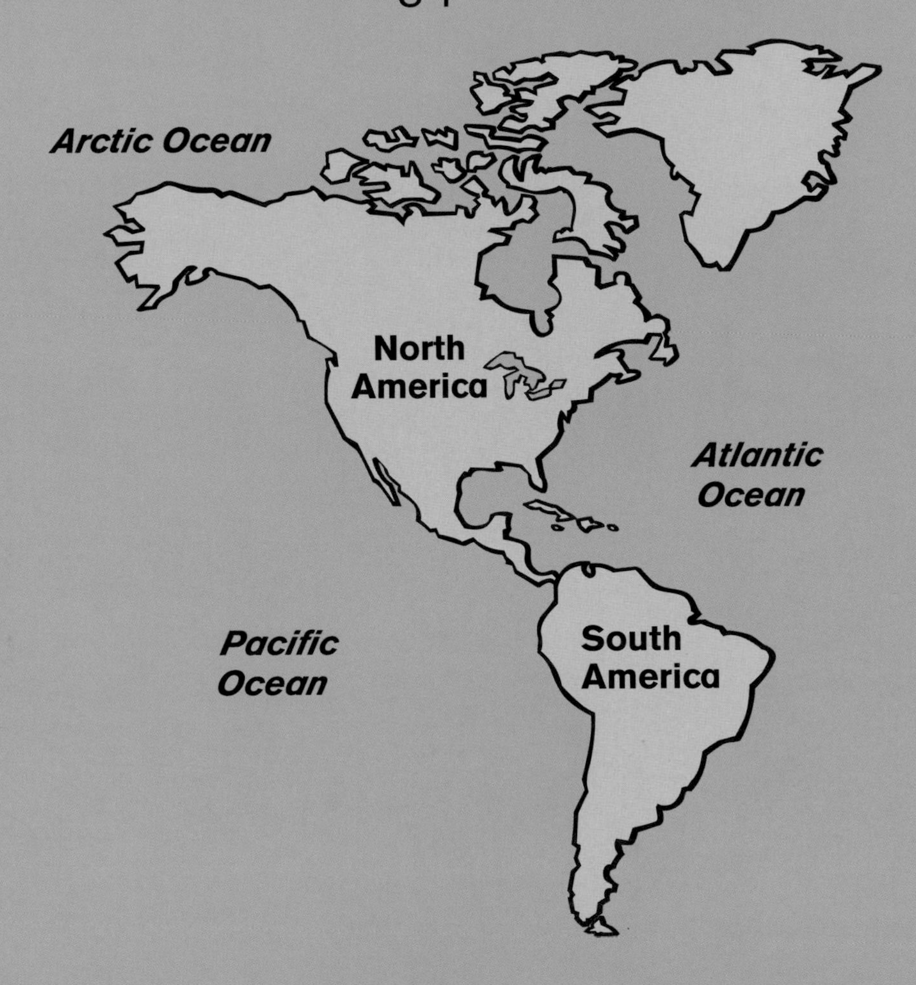


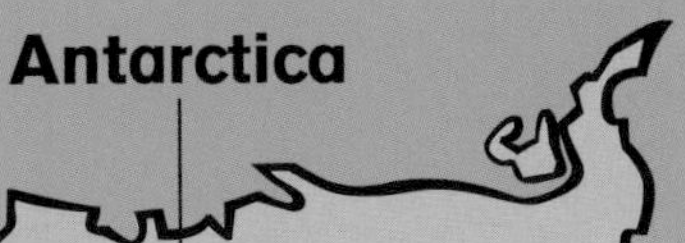

There are seven continents on Earth. Europe is the second smallest.

Water surrounds Europe on three sides, or **coasts.** The coasts curve in and out.

The curvy coasts give fishing boats many places to dock.

People visit
the beaches
on the coasts
in the summer.

Europe ends at the Ural Mountains. These low mountains rise between Europe and the continent of Asia.

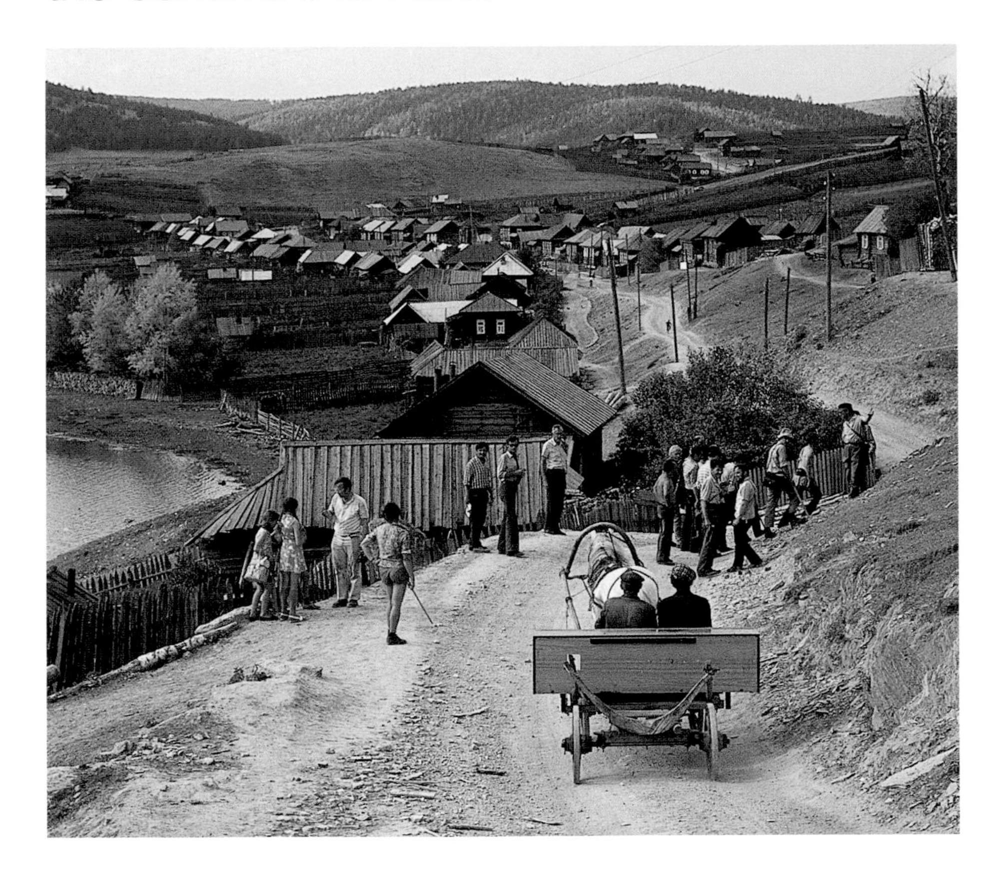

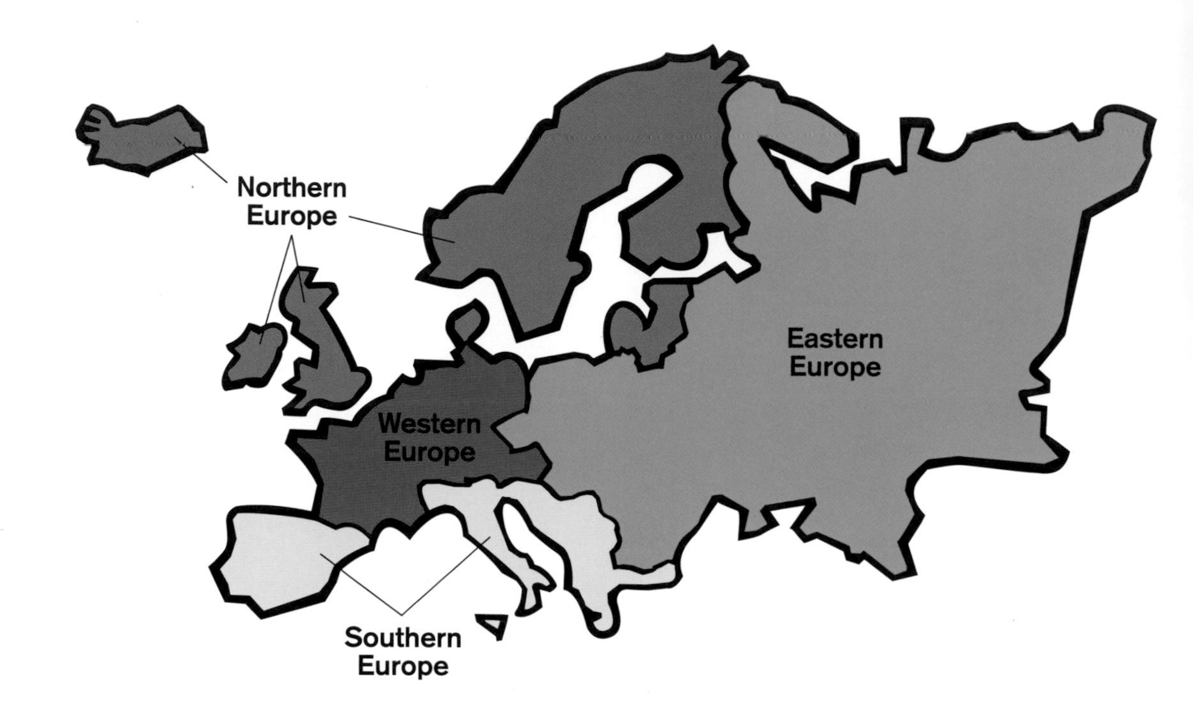


Europe has four **regions.** They are Northern Europe, Western Europe, Eastern Europe and Southern Europe.

The continent also includes many islands. The island of Iceland is part of Northern Europe.

Europe is made up of forty-seven **countries.** Russia is the biggest. It lies in Eastern Europe. Russia's grasslands are huge!

Vatican City is the world's smallest country. It is part of Southern Europe.

Mountains stretch across Northern and Southern Europe.

Whoosh! Lots of skiers go to the Alps of Southern Europe in the winter.

Between the mountains lies a huge area of **plains.**

Farmers plant wheat and other crops in the plains.

Europe's many
rivers cross the
continent.

The rivers give people and **cargo** ways to travel. This ship is on the River Rhine.

More than 700 million people live in Europe. They belong to different **ethnic groups.**

These groups speak different languages. They even support different football teams!

Do you remember the fast train? It is called the ***TGV.*** Trains bring people to Europe's many cities.

Most Europeans live and work in these cities. This is Florence, Italy, in Southern Europe.

Whoa! The Eiffel Tower rises high in Paris, France. France is the largest country in Western Europe.

Colourful Saint
Basil's Cathedral
is a famous
building in
Moscow, Russia.

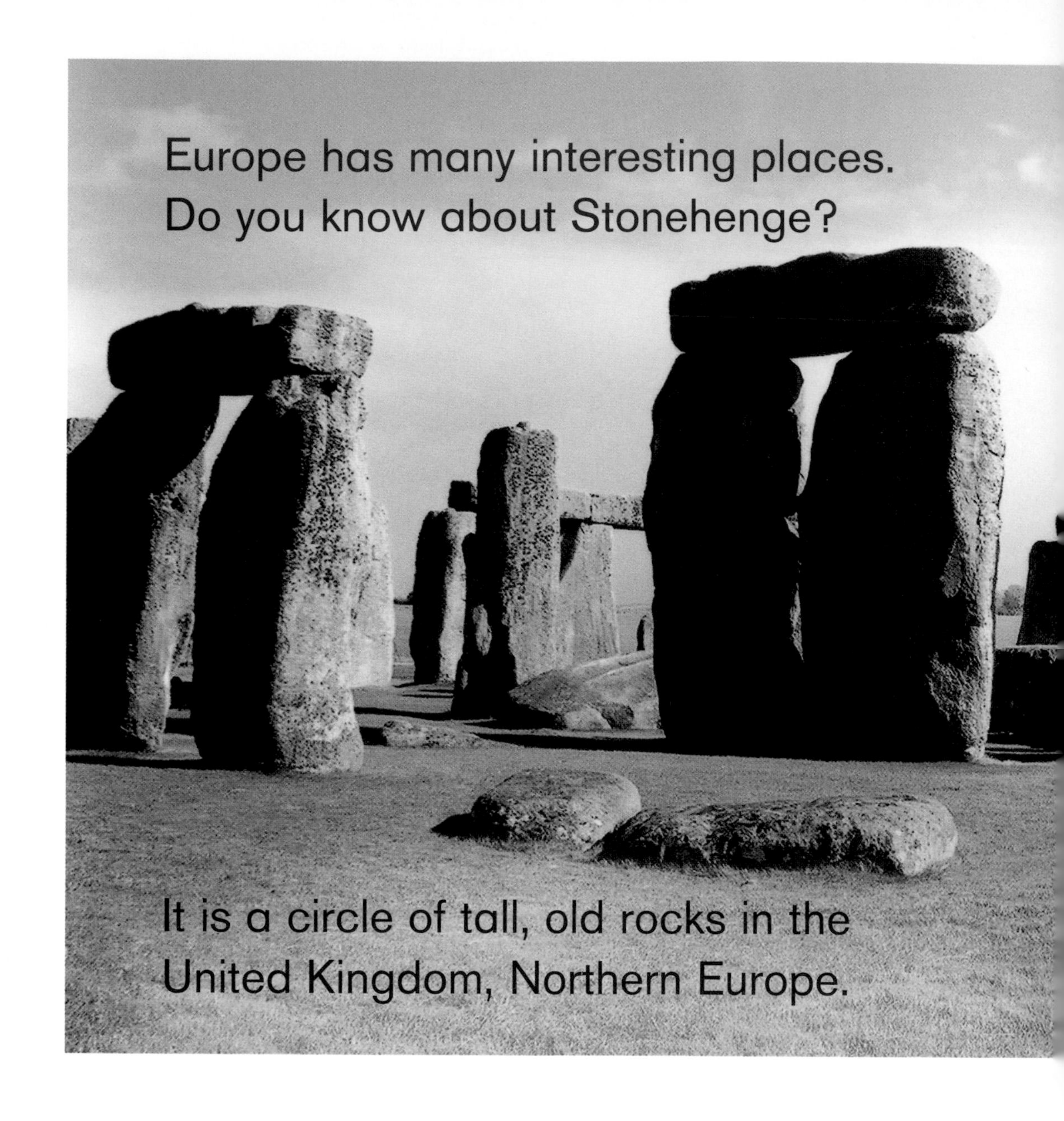

Europe has many interesting places.
Do you know about Stonehenge?

It is a circle of tall, old rocks in the
United Kingdom, Northern Europe.

There's always something new to learn about Europe!

# Facts about Europe

- Europe covers about 10 million square kilometres (4 million square miles). It is the second smallest continent after Australia.
- The main islands of Europe are Great Britain Iceland, Corsica, Crete, Ireland and Sicily.
- The main rivers of Europe are the River Volga, the River Don, the River Danube, the River Rhine, the River Po, and the River Rhône.
- More than 700 million people live in Europe.
- The people of Europe speak more than fifty languages.
- The large cities of Europe include Amsterdam, Athens, Berlin, Brussels, Budapest, Copenhagen, Dublin, Lisbon, London, Madrid, Moscow, Oslo, Paris, Rome, Stockholm and Vienna.

# Map of Europe

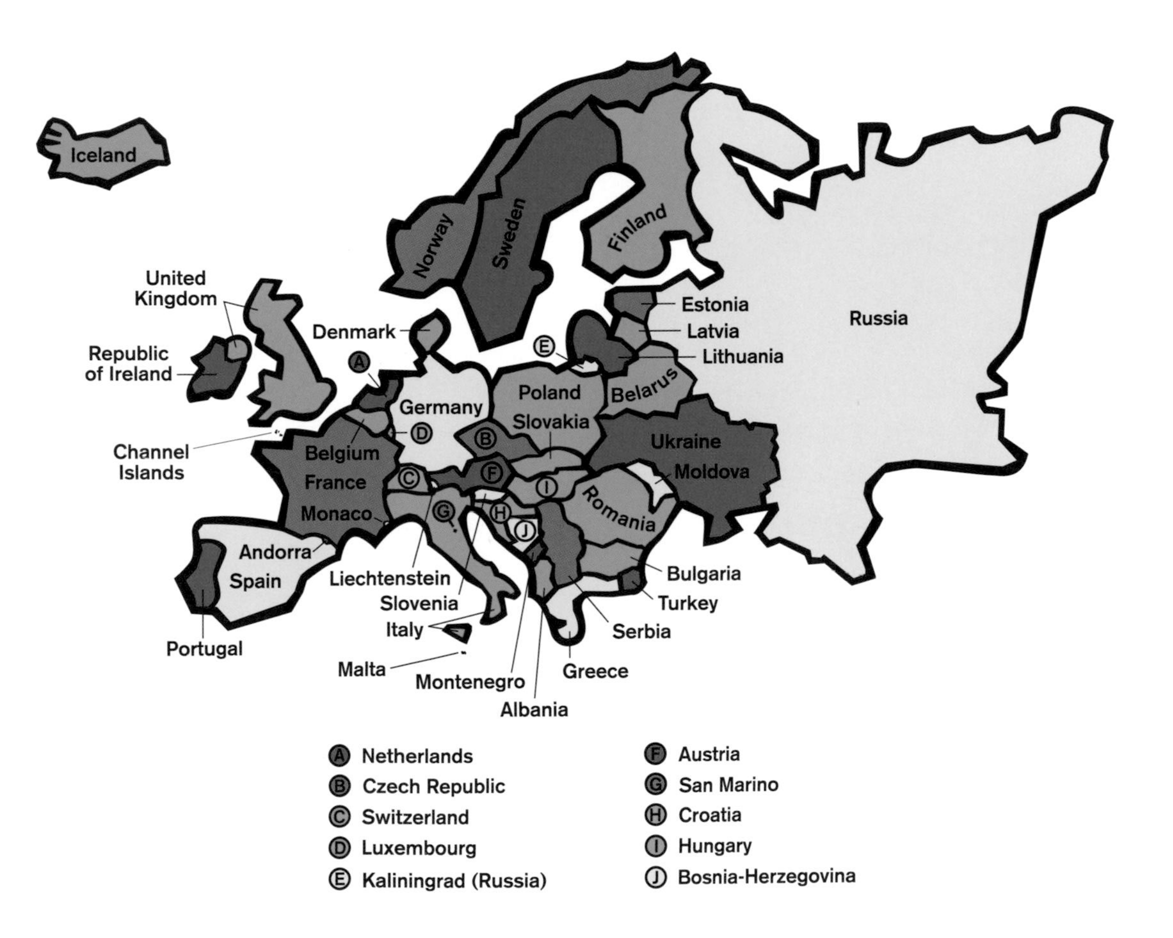

Iceland

Norway

Sweden

Finland

Russia

United Kingdom

Denmark

Estonia

Latvia

Lithuania

Republic of Ireland

Ⓐ

Ⓔ

Poland

Belarus

Channel Islands

Germany

Ⓓ

Slovakia

Ⓑ

Ukraine

Belgium

Ⓒ

Ⓕ

Moldova

France

Ⓘ

Monaco

Ⓖ

Ⓗ

Romania

Ⓙ

Andorra

Liechtenstein

Bulgaria

Spain

Slovenia

Turkey

Italy

Serbia

Portugal

Malta

Montenegro

Greece

Albania

Ⓐ Netherlands     Ⓕ Austria

Ⓑ Czech Republic     Ⓖ San Marino

Ⓒ Switzerland     Ⓗ Croatia

Ⓓ Luxembourg     Ⓘ Hungary

Ⓔ Kaliningrad (Russia)     Ⓙ Bosnia-Herzegovina

# Glossary

**cargo:** goods that are carried on or in a ship

**coasts:** the shores, or edges, of land that are touched by water

**continent:** one of seven big pieces of land on Earth

**countries:** places where people live and share the same laws

**ethnic groups:** people who have many things in common. They might speak the same language or follow the same religion.

**plains:** flat areas of land often used as farmland

**regions:** small parts of a larger piece of land

***TGV:*** letters that stand for the French words *train à grand vitesse,* or high-speed train

# Further Reading and Website

**Books**

Bell, Rachael. *Ireland* (A Visit to...) Heinemann Library, 2000.

Cumming, David. *Greece* (Letters from Around the World) Cherrytree Books, 2005.

Fischer, Teresa. *France* (Food and Festivals) Raintree, 1999.

Foster, Leila. *Europe* (Heinemann First Library: Continents) Heinemann Library, 2007.

Goodman, Polly. *Sweden* (Letters from Around the World) Cherrytree Books, 2007.

Pirotta, Saviour. *A Flavour of Italy* (Food and Festivals) Hodder Wayland, 1999.

Powell, Jillian. *Great Britain* (Looking at Countries) Franklin Watts, 2006.

Powell, Jillian. *Russia* (Looking at Countries) Franklin Watts, 2006.

Powell, Jillian. *Spain* (Looking at Countries) Franklin Watts, 2006.

Powell, Jillian. *What's It Like to Live in France?* (What's It Like to Live in) Hodder Wayland, 2003.

Senker, Cath. *Germany* (Letters from Around the World) Cherrytree Books, 2005.

**Enchanted Learning**

http://enchantedlearning.com/geography/europe

The geography section of this website has links to every continent.

# Index